# If They Mated ?

BY
Conan O'Brien
Robert Smigel
Andy Richter
Louis C. K.
Ned Goldreyer
Michael Gordon
Jonathan Groff
Marsh McCall
Brian Reich
David Reynolds
Dino Stamatopoulos
Michael Stoyanov
Mike Sweeney

HYPERION
NEW YORK

**Celebrity Photos Supplied by:**
AP/Wide World

Gus Buters

Celebrity Photo Agency

Marion Ettlinger

Focus on Sports, Inc.

FPG

Globe Photos, Inc.

Mark Scott/LGI Photo Agency

Movies Star News

Czvekus, Granitz, Marzullo, Pag/Stills, Spellman/Retna

Big Pictures, Kaplin, Pictorial, Pulin, SF, Shaw, Zuffante/Star File

Andonson, Banks, Bourguet, Cates, De Lafosse, Fineman, Kirkland, Kraft,
Maiman, Prigent, Robert, Stone, Tannenbaum, Trapper/Sygma

Leslie Weiner

For information address Hyperion, 114 Fifth Avenue, New York, New York 10011.

**Packagers:** Leigh Anne Brodsky and Anthony Knight

**Interior Design and Production:** Robert Bull Design

Library of Congress Cataloging-In-Publication Data
ISBN 0-7868-8156-9
First Edition
10 9 8 7 6 5 4 3 2 1

# ACKNOWLEDGMENTS

Show Artist: Kevin Frank

Show Graphic Art Director: Anne Elbaqali

Photo Research: Charlie Wilke

Special Thanks:

Geoffry Addeo
Susan Beckett
Dana Calderwood
Jonathan Flom
Gabrielle Heyman
Anthony Knight
Liz Plonka
Peter Seligman

Maysie Anderson
Mike Bosze
Brendan Connor
Megan Gaynor
John Irwin
Jennifer Konawal
Jeff Ross
Jessica Sklar

Ellie Barancik
Leigh Anne Brodsky
Eric Ellenbogen
Jim Henry
Tracy King
Nanette Marks
Mitch Salem
George Stephanopoulos

Show Photography:
Norman Ng
Leslie Weiner

Packagers:
Leigh Anne Brodsky
Anthony Knight

# FOREWORD

—Conan O'Brien

This is a very exciting project for all of us here at *Late Night*. As you know, there's a long history of paperback books based on TV shows. In 1939, shortly after the first televised picture was broadcast from WNBT studios (an image of Felix the Cat), a paperback book hit the stands entitled *The Image of Felix the Cat*. Because it was the Depression, most copies of the book were eaten.

My happiest childhood memories are of my father reading me to sleep from the paperback *Gomer Says Hey* or its successful follow-up, *Pyle Get Back Here!* I firmly believe that my dog-eared copy of *The Match Game '75 Companion* helped get me through the lonely periods of my adolescence. Even now, in moments of crisis, I come back to it.

That said, I'd like to take a moment to address the celebrities depicted in these pages. Maybe my perspective is a little different than yours, but I don't think you should be offended. It seems to me these images are very flattering. Were I you, I'd want to cut out my photos and display them on my mantel long before I chose to take legal action. But maybe you were brought up differently.

In closing, I'd like to thank former Mayor Ed Koch and Abe Vigoda (*The Godfather*, *Fish*) for their generous financial assistance. Sometimes words aren't enough.

# FOREWORD

—Robert Smigel

On behalf of all the *Late Night with Conan O'Brien* writers, I'd like to thank you for your purchase of our first book, *If They Mated*. As you scan the contents of *If They Mated*, you will notice that *If They Mated* is essentially made up of doctored, "morphed," photographs. The question may arise, then, as to why thirteen writers are required for such a book. All the jokes, per se, are inherent in the photographs. One might even suggest that *If They Mated* writes itself. An argument could be made that, perhaps, the cover should read *If They Mated* by *If They Mated*. Well, let's see *If They Mated* ride a bicycle, or make a barbecue. Let's see *If They Mated* beat me at bowling. Get the picture? Back off. Seriously. You're really beginning to annoy me. The fact is, a lot of work goes into choosing the people who mate with the people that they're seeing at the time. Look, I don't have to explain myself. I wrote "Da Bears," I deserve my name on a book. And the other writers wrote other things.

The writers would very much like to thank Brent Forrester, who came up with the concept of *If They Mated*. No, he's not a member of the writing staff. He's a writer we tried to get, but he took a job at *The Simpsons*. Anyway, he was visiting our office one day, and he gave us the idea. We're all very sorry for living.

The important thing is it's a good book (or so I'm told) and we're proud to be a part of it. And on behalf of all the writers, I would like to thank my parents, my sister, Bellanca, and, of course, my wife, Michelle. I know the entire staff would like me to say "Hi" to my two nephews, Russell and Erik. Hi, you guys. What do you have there? A bucket? Cool. Of course, we would be remiss not to mention that I'm selling my 1989 Volvo. There's a little rust on the body but the interior's in mint condition. And, finally, I know the writers would hate me if I didn't mention that gun control is inherently unconstitutional. At least I think so. I'm sure they all agree.

# FOREWORD

—Carl "Oldy" Olson

I ate a mash potato today. Look at all the people. Tomorow I hope I eat soup. White Stockings! White Stockings! White, White Stockings! (*laughs maniacally, wheezes*).

# If They Mated
?

C: I thought what we should do tonight, since it promises to be such a good show, is one of our favorite bits of all time. Tonight, we're doing another installment of "If They Mated." Now, this is where we take celebrity couples, and, using very advanced computer technology, we find out what their offspring might look like.

A: Right. The kind of technology that should be curing diseases.

C: I know.

A: Instead, we're using it for comedy's sake.

C: That's right, all this technology and money could have gone to something to help mankind.

A: Whoops.

C: What's become of this country?

A: I don't know.

C: Ah, screw it. Well, let's take a look at our first "If They Mated," it's Brooke Shields and Andre Agassi.

A: A very hot celebrity couple.

C: Yes, thank you, Andy. Now let's use this advanced technology right now and see what would happen . . .

C: All right . . .
A: The kid should wear a bandana.
C: It got Brooke's eyebrows, though, that's important.

. . All right, let's continue with this. It's Kim Basinger and Alec Baldwin. Both very attractive people. I'm sure their child would be nothing but . . .

C: Gee, I would not have guessed that. Okay, let's take a look at Jeff Goldblum and Laura Dern. They're a well-known celebrity couple, and let's see what their child . . .

C: Okay, let's ah, moving right along . . .
A: Nice bonnet, anyway.
C: Yes, it's a well-dressed child.

. . . Moving right along, Oh, what are you groaning for? We haven't done anything yet.

This is, of course, Maury Povich and Connie Chung, who've adopted a child, but who knows . . . let's take a look and see—

C: Ah . . . very nice looking. See, you had no reason to be upset.

A: Yeah. It was a happy face, after all.

10

C: All right, next up, Whoopi Goldberg and her new husband, we don't know his name, but they're very happy, so what if these two have a child, what can we expect?

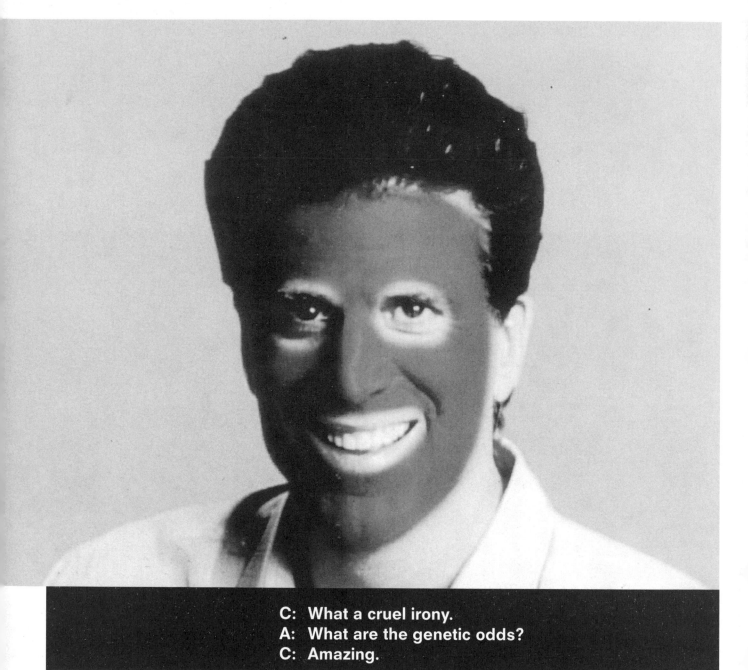

. . . Now let's look at some classy, more established celebrity couples.
Here's Ted Turner and Jane Fonda. Maybe it's too late for them,
but let's check it out . . .

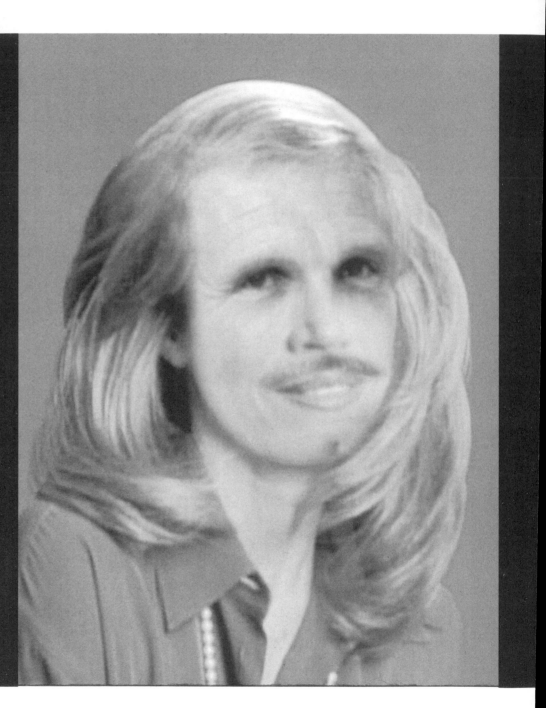

A: Oooh, my.
C: Very nice. If she shaves, not a bad looking woman.
A: Are you sure it's a she?
C: Yes, yes, we did genetic testing.
A: Oh, all right.

**C: Let's get right into the next couple**, Maria Shriver and Arnold **Schwarzenegger. I think they ha**ve some kids, but let's see what **they might look like grown-up . . .**

A: Whose jaw is that?
C: All it's missing is neckbolts.
A: Yeah, just a guess, but I think it sounds like this . . . Aaarrrrrr!
C: Mom, I want food!!!

. . . Moving right along, here's
another classy pair,
Dennis Quaid and Meg Ryan.
Let's find out what
would happen . . .

C: All right, here's a big couple, they've recently separated, but I think it's just temporary . . .

A: Oh yeah. These two were made for each other.

C: It's Liz Taylor, and what's his name, it's Larry Fortensky, I think.

A: Larry Fortensky, yes.

C: My card says Jeff Fortensky, that's the kind of show we're running.  Okay, let's see what their child might look like . . .

A: Ozzy!

C: It is . . . it's actually Ozzy Osbourne.

A: This whole section has an eighth grade theme to it.

C: All right. In the interest of science, we'll move on to Oprah Winfrey and her longtime fiancé Stedman Graham. Now, these, I don't believe they have a child, so let's see what would happen "If They Mated" . . .

C: I think that's a very handsome man. I don't know why people react the way they do.
A: Childish. The whole audience is childish.

C: All right, now here's a very glamorous on-and-off couple, Daryl Hannah and JFK, Jr. Maybe they'll never wind up together, but wouldn't it be great? Let's see what their child would look like . . .

A: That child is drunk!
C: I guess they shouldn't mate.

. . . Okay, right now let's take a look at some rock'n'roll couples.

A: I love rock'n'roll couples.

C: Good support there, Andy. Okay, we'll start with that old standby,
Mick Jagger and Jerry Hall. Now, these guys have children,
but our technology can show us what they'll look like grown up . . .

A: It's Steven Tyler.

C: Steven Tyler from Aerosmith, yes. All right, now we know where Steven Tyler comes from.

Okay, let's take a look now at Iman and David Bowie.
Let's see what would happen if . . .

C: Very attractive. Very, very attractive.

A: Looks like a candy of some sort.

C: Yes it does. Now our next rock 'n'roll couple is Winona Ryder and David Pirner. He's from . . .

A: Soul Asylum.

C: Soul Asylum. This couple is very hot right now. What if they have a child . . .

C: You know, the good thing about that child is that it will have incredible night vision.

A: Mmmm hmm.

C: Okay, now we're going to take a look at Rod Stewart and his supermodel wife, Rachel Hunter. I don't know why you're booing at all. We're going to see, maybe these two have a child already, what might it look like if the child matures . . .

C: Now, folks, I myself thought
that wasn't good enough,
so I had them put a pirate
hat on the child, just for my
own amusement.

C: I know that's cheating, but I reserve the right to do what I want.
A: There was something definitely nautical about that kid.
C: Yes there was . . . What the hell are you talking about?
A: There's people out there who know what I mean.
C: They're all watching cable, though.

. . . All right, let's wrap up this section with a big tabloid couple. *Baywatch* star Pamela Anderson and rocker Tommy Lee. They always say that before his name.

A: Rocker Tommy Lee.

C: Rocker, it's like
one long name,
Rocker Tommy Lee.
Anyway, they
haven't had a child
yet, but they will
soon, I'm sure. Let's
look into the future
and see
what that child
will look like . . .

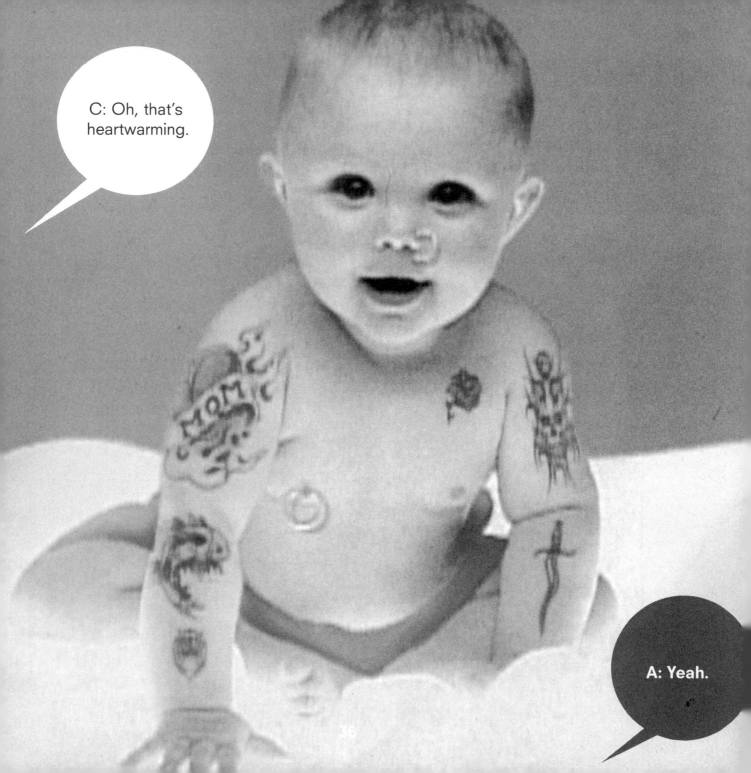

C: Yes. Well, Andy, this is all fun and good, but it's important sometimes to look back on some of the great celebrity couples of recent years that could've mated, but didn't. We call this section "If They Had Mated."

A: If only they had mated.

C: Yes, very sad. Okay, let's start with one of the all-time beautiful couples, Cindy Crawford and Richard Gere. Surely their kid would've been . . .

C: Wow.
A: Damn mole gene.
C: Tough break.

. . . Okay, now here's a truly great couple from the recent past, Madonna and Charles Barkley. Before Dennis Rodman, before Rosie O'Donnell, there were these two.

A: The real deal.

C: Exactly. Now what kind of offspring would they have produced?

A: Whoa.
C: There we go.
A: Their kid would've ripped the Cindy Crawford kid's head off.

C: Now we come to one of the most-talked-about couples of recent times: Hugh Grant and Divine Brown.  In their brief time together, we're pretty sure they didn't mate. But what if they had?
A: Had they only . . .

A: Wow.
C: It's the computer, ladies and gentlemen. It's out of my hands.

. . . Now, of course, we would be remiss to do "If They Had Mated" without including Roseanne and Tom Arnold. These two actually tried to mate, at least, and now we can see the child they would've had.

C: Only the best technology.
A: How does the computer know?
C: The computer is right 98% of the time.

. . . Okay, lets look at some happier couples, ones that you just know will mate someday. Here's a big one, Tom Cruise and Nicole Kidman.

A: Cruise. He did that Dracula movie, right?

C: You know who he is, Andy. All right, what gorgeous child would these two produce?

C: Not bad.
   I'd still run
   my fingers
   through
   its hair.
A: Nah. He
   looked better
   as Dracula.
C: Yeah, you're
   right.

C: Okay, here's Kenneth Branagh, who directed *Frankenstein*, that's for segue fans, and his wife, the enchanting Oscar-winner Emma Thompson. These two have it all.

A: Conan, they just recently split up.

C: Oh. Right. Well, maybe if we show their potential child, they'll get back together . . .

C: I'm attracted to that person.
A: I think this child got the best features of both.
C: I think so, too. I don't know why people are so upset.

. . . Now here's another happy longtime couple,
Danny DeVito and Rhea Perlman. They may have kids,
but what if the child matures? We need to know . . .

C: I think that kid's lovable.
A: Sure. You wanna buy it a drink and put it in a taxi.
C: You do.

. . . Now this next couple's been together for years, albeit on and off — Don Johnson and Melanie Griffith. They're split, but could get back together any minute, so let's speculate . . .

C: Maybe they won't get back together.

Okay, we spoke about Roseanne, it's only fair we bring up her new husband whom she's very happy with, Ben Thomas who, is he related to you?

A: I . . . you know, at the reunions, I am in no shape to figure out who's who.

C: Okay, well it could be . . . it could be your older brother Ben, anyway, these two just had a kid, so let's see, almighty computer, what we can expect . . .

C: Hi there. And it's loose in the city!!!

. . . All right, moving along, of course, this is all scientific truth, ladies and gentlemen, so don't think we're making any judgments. This is Yasir Arafat and his wife. Many people didn't think Yasir Arafat would ever get married.

A: He finally gave in.

C: Right. Now he and his lovely wife will surely produce a child, if they haven't already . . .

C: Isn't that nice . . . cute kid.
A: Looks friendly, too.

C: All right, we're gonna look now at, I love these two, these two are very close to my heart. I'm talking, of course, about the Taster's Choice™ couple.

Now, of course, in the famous coffee ads, they're always flirting. It's all very sexy, but what happens when they finally get together and have a kid?

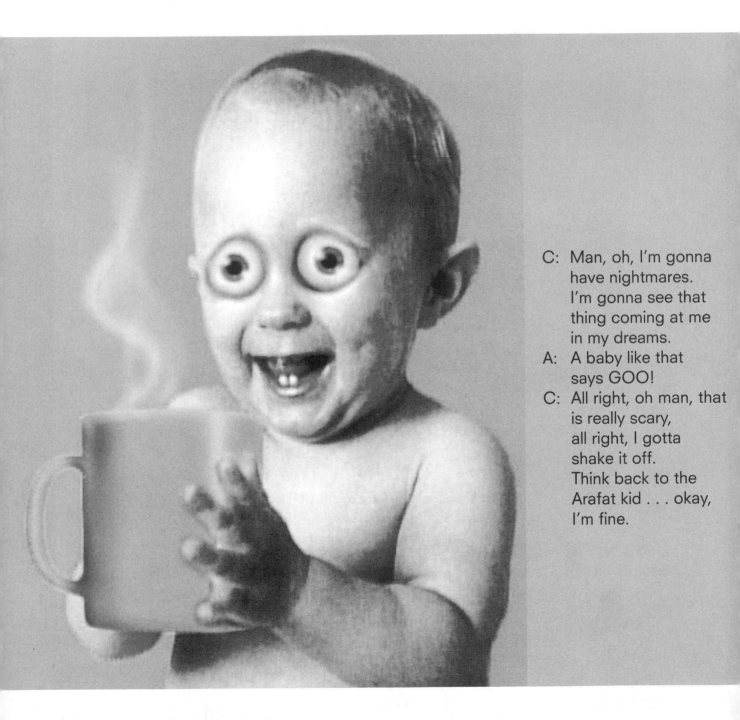

C: Man, oh, I'm gonna
have nightmares.
I'm gonna see that
thing coming at me
in my dreams.
A: A baby like that
says GOO!
C: All right, oh man, that
is really scary,
all right, I gotta
shake it off.
Think back to the
Arafat kid . . . okay,
I'm fine.

. . . Okay, moving on, what about Ben and Jerry?   Now these are two guys, so they can't have a child, nor would they want to, but what if they did, what could we . . . ?

C: What are we saying with that?
A: I guess there's a double for everyone in the world.
C: See, we learn here.

60

. . . Now, while we're on a sort of surreal plane here with Ben
and Jerry, let's explore some more pairs of people that we'd
all like to see mate, but they just can't, or won't.

A: A "Fantasy If They Mated."

C: Exactly. Let's start with two people that I think everyone
would want to see mate: Marcia Clark and Robert Shapiro.
C'mon, we sat through that trial. It's the least they could do.

A: You know you've thought about it.

C: Of course they have. Well, imagine no longer . . .

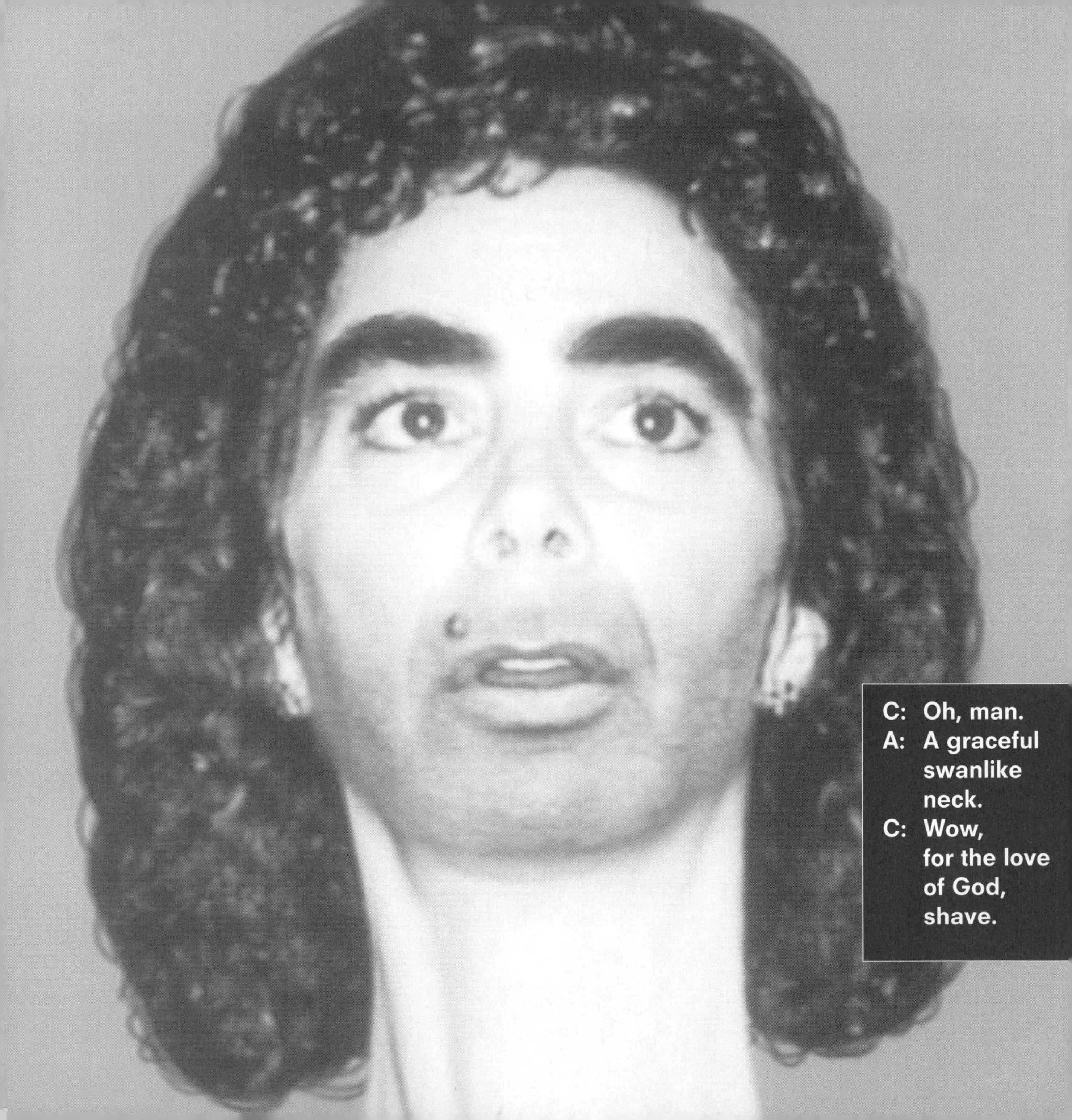

C: Oh, man.
A: A graceful swanlike neck.
C: Wow, for the love of God, shave.

. . . All right, here's another pair that we'll never get to see mate, but imagine the possibilities: Newt Gingrich and Hillary Clinton.

A: I think there's a chance
   for these two.
C: Really? To get together?
A: Sure.  They've got that sexual tension going.
C: Like on "Moonlighting."
A: Exactly.  Will they or won't they?
C: Maybe you're right.  Well, we can't wait that
   long.  Let's see what would happen.

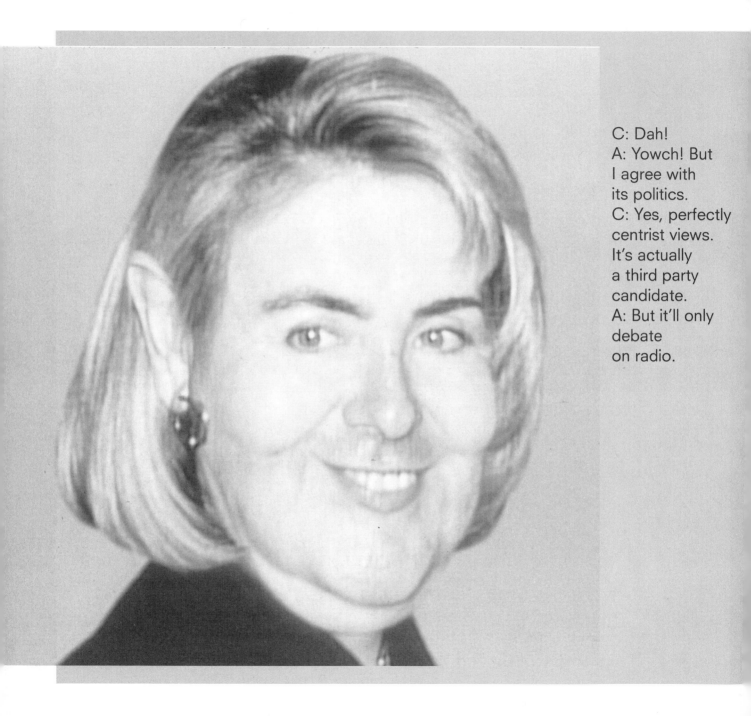

C: Dah!
A: Yowch! But
I agree with
its politics.
C: Yes, perfectly
centrist views.
It's actually
a third party
candidate.
A: But it'll only
debate
on radio.

C: All right, continuing now with another fantasy couple, Regis and Kathie Lee. They're not involved, of course, but a lot of people write me and say, "Gee, Conan, what do you think their child might look like?" So let's find out . . .

C: They're good people. It's not a reflection on them, it's just a genetic lottery.

A: The progeny is every bit as darling as they are.
C: Yes! We used the word "progeny"; we get four points.

. . . Okay, here's two people who haven't been really thought of as a couple, but what if it happened? I'm talking about sumo wrestler Konishiki and superwaif model Kate Moss. What would happen if these two got together?

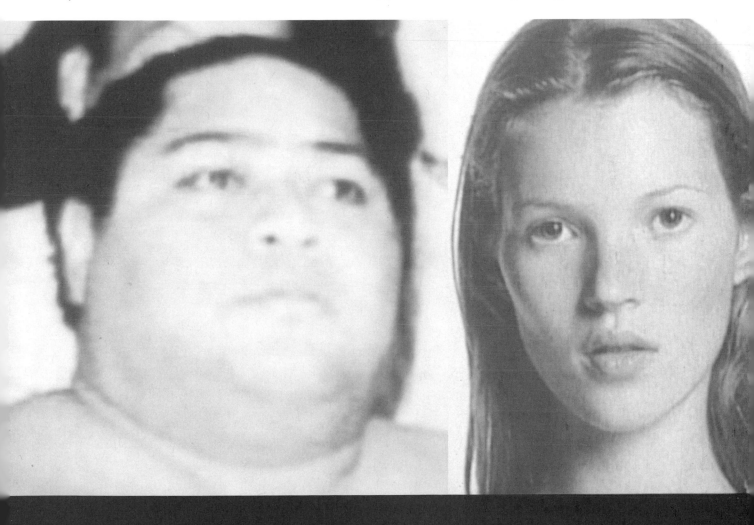

C: Well, it's kinda true.  See, that's information Kate Moss can use.

A:  Stay away Kate Moss, stay away.

C: I hope she's watching.

. . . All right, here we go, here's a dream couple anyone would be curious about about, the venerable Lassie and the dog on *Frasier*.

A:  Lassie could teach that dog a thing or two.

C:  Yes. She's been there and back. So what would happen if these two should mate?

C: Oh, man.
A: Wow!
C: I wish we had a lawyer on the set right now. Ladies and gentleman, this is just computer technology. Andy and I had nothing to do with this. *Blame the computer*. Okay.

. . . Now while we're talking about TV shows, let's consider Mike and Carol Brady. Now, keep in mind, these two never had a child together, just very lovely girls and boys on their own. What if they had actually had sex, and, consequently, a child?

C: Look, Alice is in the mid-
   dle still. Wow.
A: It's a miracle.

72

. . . Now, here's one more fantasy couple, they haven't been together, but they're sort of associated, "Forrest Gump" and "Ernest."
You know, two kind of dimwitted . . .

A: A step behind.

C: Yes. Let's put them together and see what would happen if they mated.

C: I love that guy. What a happy, friendly face he has.

A: I'm told that Gump and Rain Man yields Pauly Shore.

C: That's true. Well, Andy, it's all well and good to talk about fantasy couples, but we can't forget our responsibility to speculate about the offspring of real couples.

A: It's rewarding work.

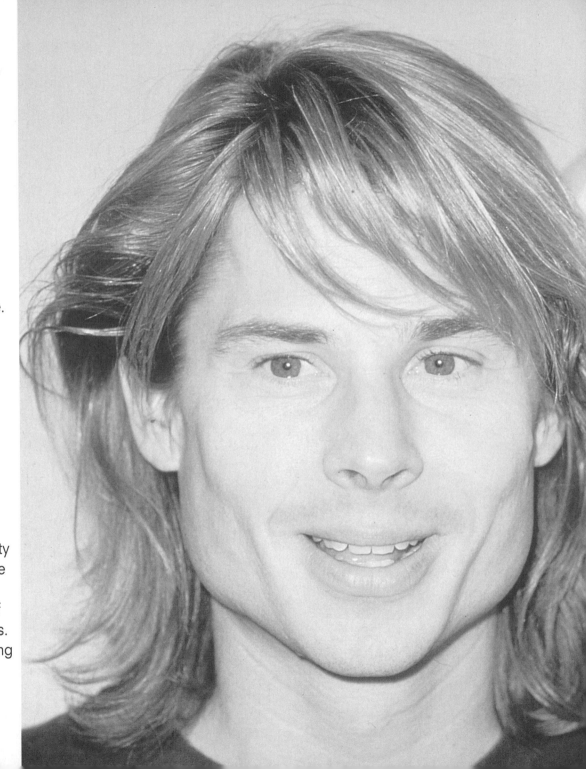

C: It's what we were put on this earth to do. So let's knock off some of the hot young couples out there right now. First, the "90210" couple, Brian Austin Greene and Tiffany Amber Theissen. This is a young, attractive couple that goes out. So "If They Mated," what could we expect?

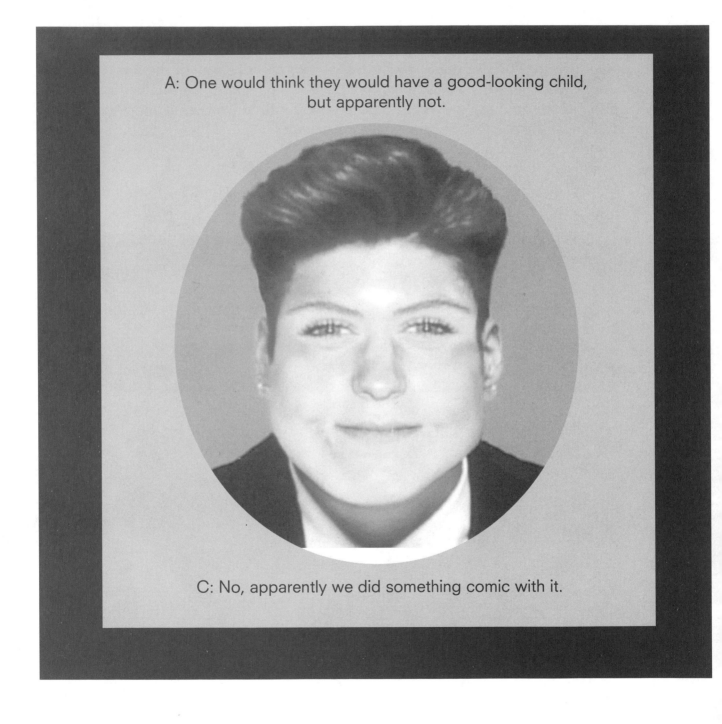

. . . All right, moving on, Nicolas Cage and Patricia Arquette. They're a really hot couple right now, aren't they? They're the ones everyone's talking about.

A: I'm talking about them.

C: You're constantly talking about them. What would happen if they mated, I want to know.

C: Oh, my Lord! Now, wait a minute! Very interesting!

A: It's oddly enough the same as you would get if you cross Christian Slater with Joel Grey.

C: There you go. We're doing so much good here.

A: So much good.

**C:** Now, one of the wildest hot young couples, we mentioned Kate Moss earlier, here she is with her actual boyfriend, Johnny Depp. Let's take a look at what their offspring would look like.

A: I sat
next to
that
person
in the
eighth
grade.
C: I think
we all
did.

. . . Okay, here's maybe the hottest couple going, it's the Sexiest Man Alive Brad Pitt and the actress Gwyneth Paltrow. Let's not waste any time.

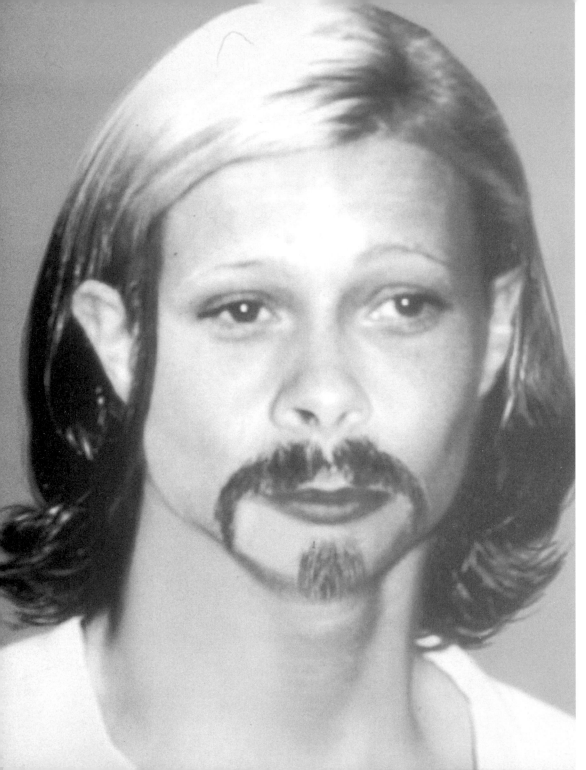

C: Boy. What a
   disappointment.
A: It's the Sexiest
   Carny Alive.
C: Right. That's no
   small honor,
   by the way.

. . . All right, let's try a very cool hot couple, Isabella Rossellini and Gary Oldman. These two, this is *Blue Velvet* meets *Sid and Nancy*, this should be interesting . . .

C: Now that's
   a cool guy.
A: Kind of
   a hip, young
   Uncle Miltie.
C: Yes. A brooding
   drag comedian.

. . . As we mentioned, Melanie Griffith is split with Don Johnson, and here she is with her new heartthrob, Latin lover Antonio Banderas. So what if they . . . did the deed?

A: "Shloonka, shloonka," I call it.

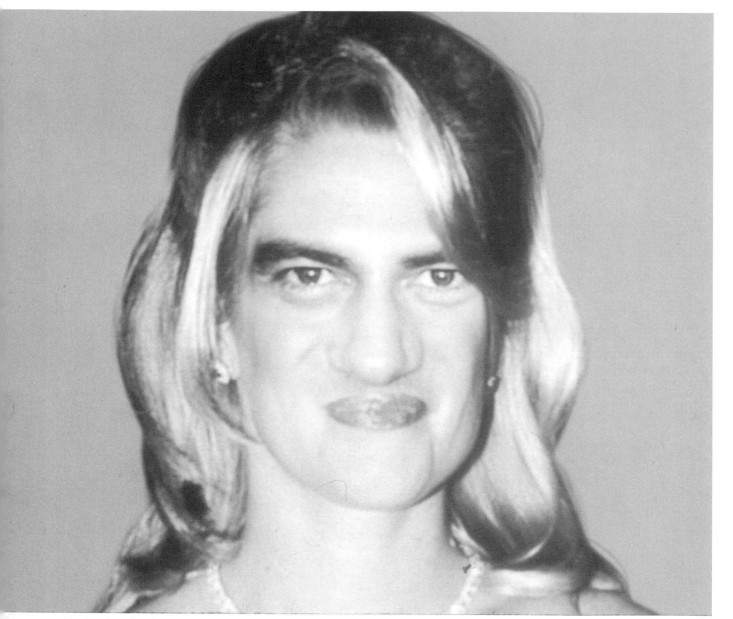

C: Hmmm. I sensed from the audience that time, at first repulsion and then, "I don't know . . .
A: " . . . yeah, I might like it."

C: Now I wouldn't exactly call this next couple young, but without a doubt they're hot. Woody Allen and Soon-Yi. And using the advanced science, we find . . .

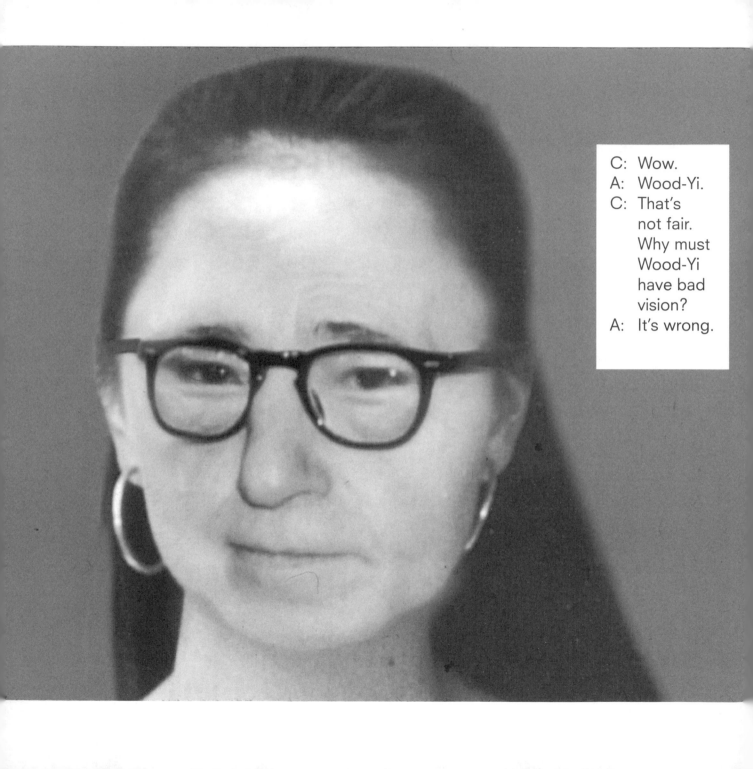

C: All right, and while we're on the subject of May-December romances, we might as well look at Anna Nicole Smith and her 90-year-old millionaire husband J. Howard Marshall II, whom she married not for the money. Now, if there was a way they could have had a child, what would we have seen . . .

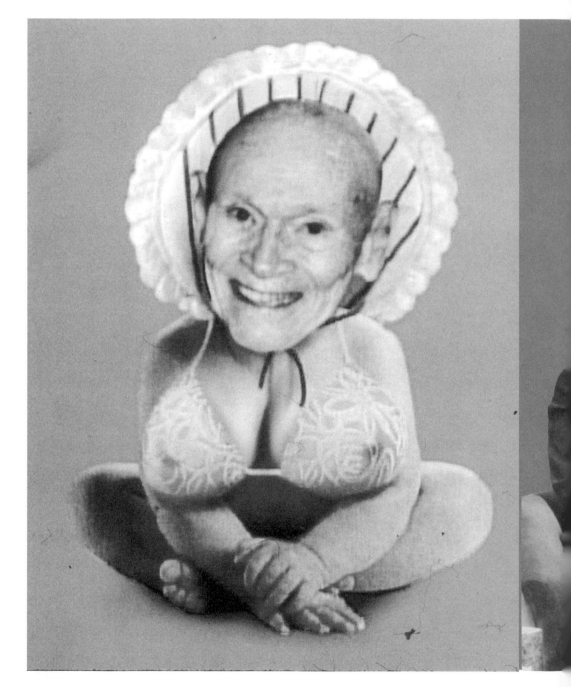

C: Wow. I feel dirty now.
A: Me likee baby.
C: Let's get the hell away from this one. Moving on . . .

. . . Y'know, with so many celebrity couples splitting up nowadays, it seems
another variation of "If They Mated" is in order. Right now, we have a special
mix-and-match edition in honor of all those celebrities breaking up.
We call it "If They Mixed and Mated."

A: If only.

C: Shut up. Okay, our first couple is Christie Brinkley, who divorced a while back
from Billy Joel, and Tom Arnold of the ubiquitous Tom and Roseanne Arnold.
What if these two had found solace and comfort in each other's arms? Then what?

A: Now, this one's sort of Milton Berle and Chastity Bono.
C: Yes. Another rumored couple, by the way.

. . . Okay, and consequently, it's only fair that we take a look at Roseanne and Billy Joel. What if these two then hooked up, maybe out of spite, maybe out of love? What would their child . . .

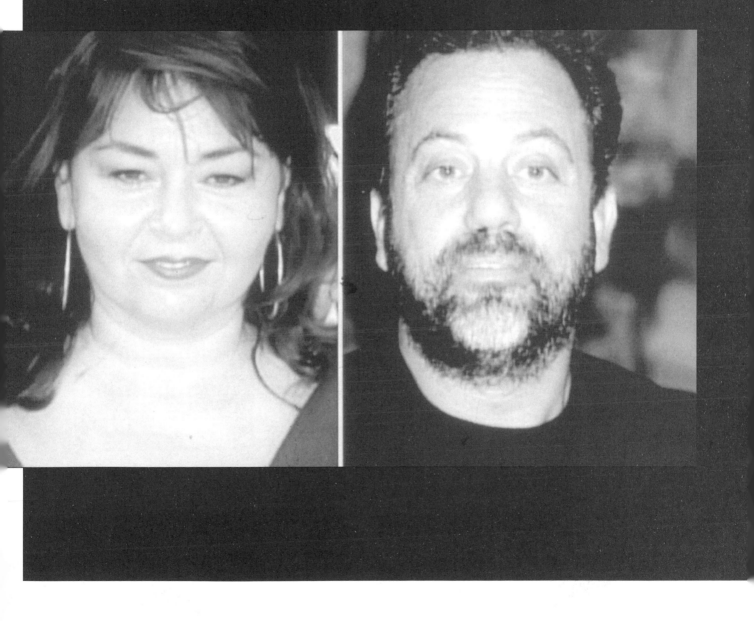

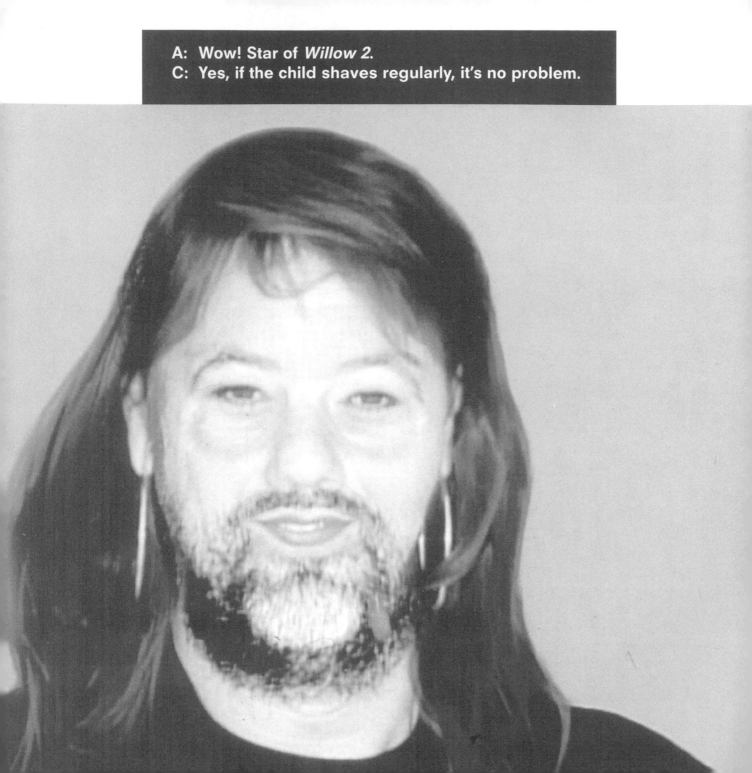

A: Wow! Star of *Willow 2*.
C: Yes, if the child shaves regularly, it's no problem.

. . . Well, let's move on to the next mix-and-match pair, Loni Anderson, ex-longtime wife of Burt Reynolds, and Ashley Hamilton, who was married for a minute to Shannen Doherty. What if, for some reason, these two got together and had a child?

C: You know, it sort of looks like one of — like the 1974 incarnation of David Bowie.

A: Yeah, David Bowie sans neck.

C: And,
of course
it follows that
Burt would
then have
a child with
Shannen
Doherty.
A child
who would
look like . . .

A   Oh, boy.
C:  Yes. Burt will be doing our show real soon.
A:  I would've guessed that the crooked eye gene was recessive,. Oh, well.

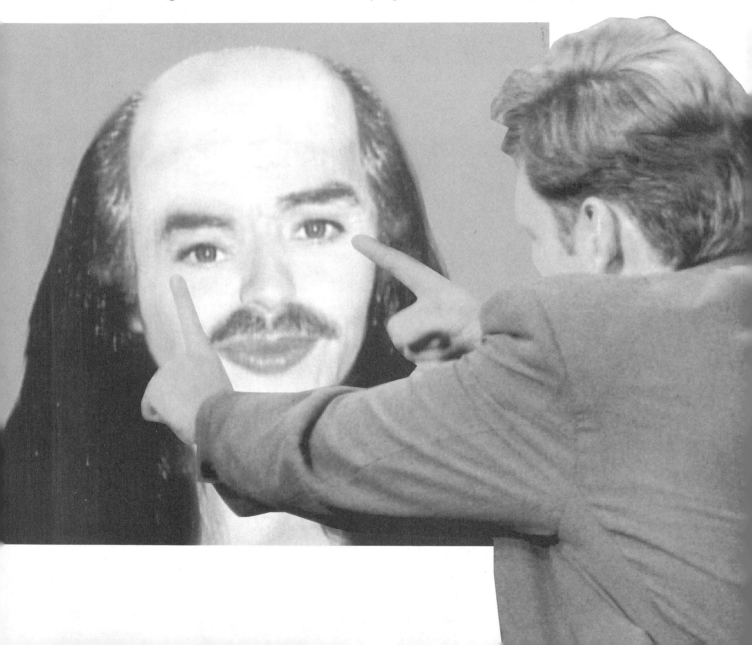

C: Well, as a capper to our "If They Mixed and Mated," it seems appropriate to match up two Hall of Famers, Johnny Carson, who's been married five times, and Liz Taylor, who's had, I don't know, twenty husbands. Maybe more, I can't remember. What kind of kid would these two have had? Now we can finally know . . .

C: That is weird, wild stuff.
A: You are correct, sir.
C: Well, that was fun, Andy. It makes me want to go check out more couples that didn't make it, or "If They Had Mated".
A: You've got more?
C: Oh, sure. I'm filled with hate.

. . . Here's a good one, Princess Diana and Major James Hewitt. They had an affair, apparently, but it didn't last. But what "If They Had Mated?"

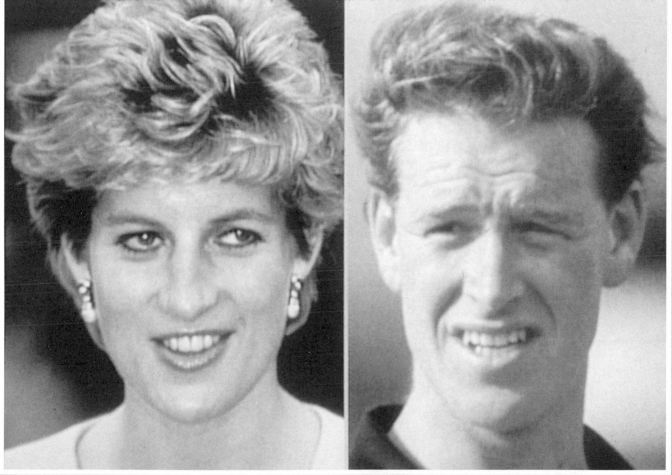

C: Oh, man, inbred royalty.
A:  Genetics can be cruel.
C:  Wow.

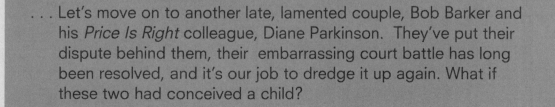

. . . Let's move on to another late, lamented couple, Bob Barker and his *Price Is Right* colleague, Diane Parkinson. They've put their dispute behind them, their embarrassing court battle has long been resolved, and it's our job to dredge it up again. What if these two had conceived a child?

C: That's the great thing about "If They Mated," we learn so much about the future, and no one gets hurt.

A: And tragic mistakes are averted.

C: We've done some good.

. . . All right, another couple that didn't work out— President Clinton and Paula Jones. We're pretty sure these two didn't have a child, but what would one have looked like? The public deserves to know . . .

C: The computer is faultless.
A: Blinding accuracy.
C: What a piece of machinery.

. . . Now, here's a very happy couple that unfortunately never mated, Betty and Barney Rubble. Remember, Bamm-Bamm was adopted. All right, so what if the Rubbles could've mated? What would their own child look like?

A: That makes an interesting point. It's saying that Newt is prehistoric.
C: That's right. Norman Lear submitted these jokes.

. . . And finally, Tonya Harding and Jeff Gillooly. We were all rooting for these kids, but it just didn't get done. Now we can only wonder what would've happened "If They Had Mated". . .

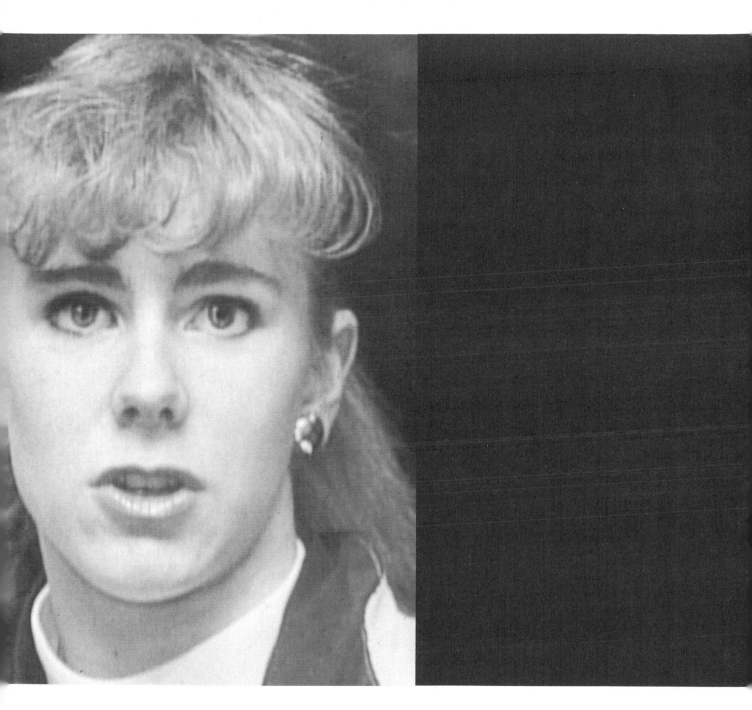

C: There you have it.

A: Question answered.

C: Thanks, science. Now there are a few more celebrity couples, Andy, that we just can't ignore without causing a huge uproar.

A: We don't want that.

C: No, we don't. Huge uproars suck.

. . . For example, we can't forget Michael Bolton and Nicolette Sheridan. Andy, there's a huge segment of the audience that literally feeds on Michael Bolton facts and information. Let's not disappoint those good people.

A: Actually looks like John Tesh's graduation photo.
C: Wow, yeah, it really does. My God, I'm glad you're here to point these things out.
A: Thanks.
C: The perspective you have from that chair is invaluable.
A: It's a magic chair, actually.
C: Don't be humble.

. . . All right, here's another couple people are obsessed with, of course, Claudia Schiffer and David Copperfield, the, uh, magic guy she's going out with. Let's take a look at their child.

C:  Oh, interesting. Has a nice look.
C:  But wait, there's more.

A: Ahhh.
C: Ahh. There we go, the whole magician thing.
A: 'Cause he's a magician.
C: Yes. Magician, he.

118

. . . All right, now another couple people can't get enough of is, of course, Sigfried and Roy. What would happen if these two, if it were humanly possible for them to spawn some kind of child? Someday it might be, maybe . . .

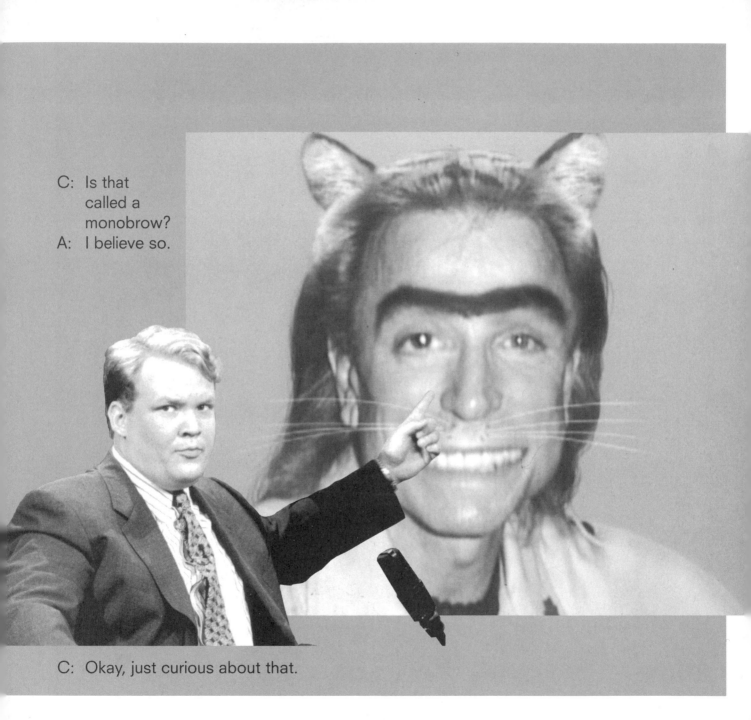

C: Is that called a monobrow?
A: I believe so.

C: Okay, just curious about that.

. . . All right. Our work is not done yet, we have more lives to ruin. Here's a couple I'm personally obsessed with, and I invite you to join me, it's Barbra Streisand and Peter Jennings, who've been spotted together at several galas.

A: *Several* galas?

C: That's right, several. You heard me. Just imagine the power a Streisand-Jennings child would have . . .

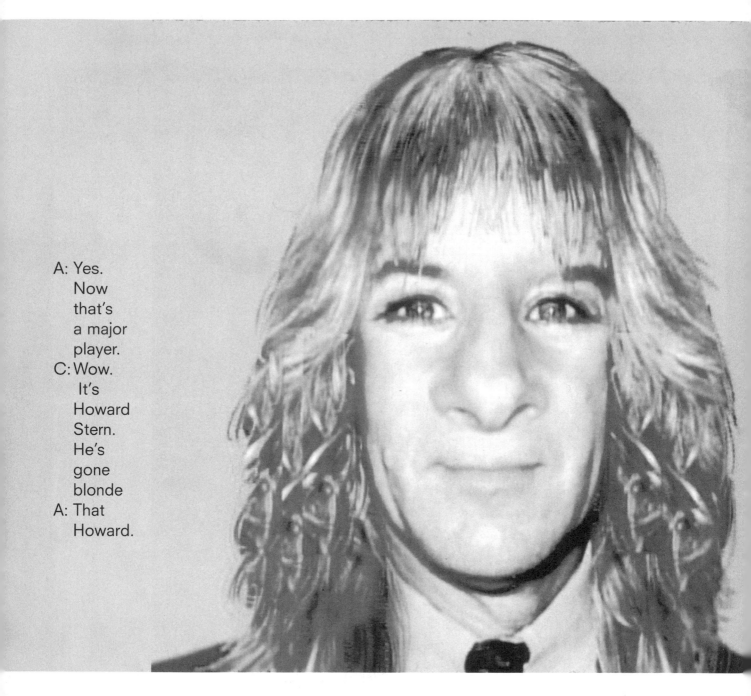

A: Yes.
   Now
   that's
   a major
   player.
C: Wow.
   It's
   Howard
   Stern.
   He's
   gone
   blonde
A: That
   Howard.

C: Okay, now just to piss people off, I thought it would be interesting to high-
light a couple that *no one* cares about.  So here's Larry King and his new
wife, is it Dorothea Lunn?  Is that right?

A: Huh?

C: There you go.  They're saying this is either his fifth . . .

A: Fifth or seventh wife, that's what they say.

C: Fifth or seventh.  Okay, no one's sure, not even Larry is sure.  Okay, what if
Larry and his new wife were to have a child . . .

C: Oh, those are very marketable, I would think.

A: (mimicking King)  Mommy, hello.

C: Where's mommy calling from?

A: (mimicking King)  Mommy from the kitchen, hello.

C: Okay, we're in the homestretch, and Andy, I feel good.  I really feel that we've done more good than harm here.  A little bit more.

A: It's a good feeling.

C: Let's wrap it up with a few more "Fantasy If They Mateds." I think these are my favorites.

A: Yes. I'll miss these most of all.

C: All right, here's a couple, it would just be great if these two got together. Princess Di and JFK, Jr. I mean, think about it. Royalty from both sides of the Atlantic. What would their child look like . . . ?

A: That's an ugly kid, but he can get a table at any restaurant in town.

C: Without a doubt. Any club—right to the head of the line.

. . . Okay, now anyone who saw *Bridges of Madison County* has got to wonder about these two— Clint Eastwood and Meryl Streep. Let's allow science to settle the question.

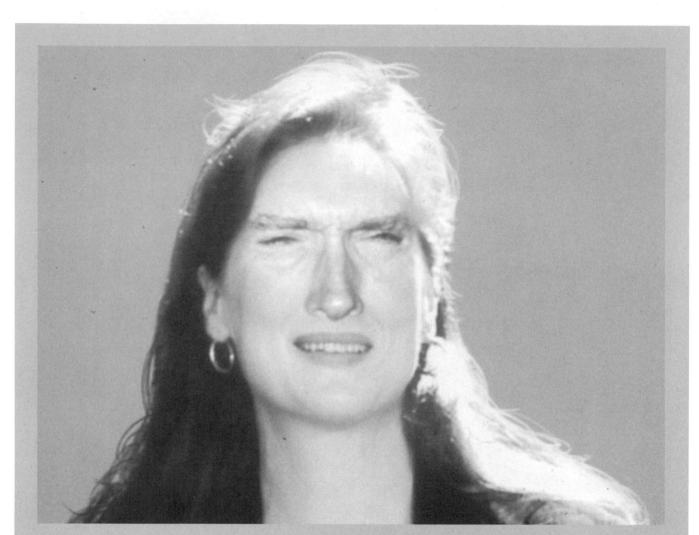

C: Oh!  Wow!  Wow!
A: Wow!
C: Amazing!  Clint's squint broke through
   the barrier.
A: I'm a little bit played.
C: Hang on, son.

. . . Now here's a great "Fantasy If They Mated," Michael Jackson
and Lisa Marie Presley.
A: Now, they are married.
C: Of course they are, but we're talking about if they *mated.*
So it's a fantasy couple.
A: Agreed.
C: Let's take a look.

C: There we go. No plastic surgeon can control the gene pool.

A: Not yet, anyway.

C: Right. There are researchers at Neverland working as we speak.

A: Huge think tanks.

C: All right, now this next one, just indulge me, folks, this is my own "Fantasy If They Mated." This is Conan O'Brien and Bridget Fonda. I don't want to start any rumors, but I'm sorry, I just really need to know. Go ahead.

C: Wow, you know what the worst part is, the child keeps the shirt I'm wearing.

A: I know, I know, sort of a Frenchman sort of look.

C: All right, my bad day at the Gap.

. . . Okay, now, Andy, I know you're happily married, but you must have a "Fantasy If They Mated" that we could share with America.

A: Well, other than my wife, the only woman I would want to have a child with is the Statue of Liberty.

C: Andy, that's very nice, that's a very nice sentiment.
Andy and the Statue of Liberty; what would happen if they mated?

C: Sorry, pal.
A: The computer's a real smart ass.

C: Here, this'll cheer you up, Andy. A great fantasy couple: Rush Limbaugh and Carnie Wilson.

A: I'm happy already.

C: See? And we haven't even seen the child. Rush and Carnie Wilson, what would we see . . . ?

C: Oh, mercy.  Thank goodness we're protected by law.
A: I love this country.

C: And wrapping it all up, what better fantasy couple, I know we've all thought about them, the gorilla from *Congo*, the hit summer movie, and the monkey from *Friends* and *Outbreak*.

A: The monkey works more, I guess.

C: Well, that's because he's real. The gorilla was a robot. But that's a whole other book. Okay, the *Congo* gorilla, the *Friends / Outbreak* monkey, what would happen "If They Mated?"

C: There. He didn't escape us.
A: We can sleep now.

C: Yes. Peace at last. Good night, folks.